FAMILY CIRCUS®

BABY ON BOARD

Bil Keane

FAWCETT GOLD MEDAL • NEW YORK

A Fawcett Gold Medal Book
Published by Ballantine Books
Copyright © 1989 by Bil Keane, Inc.
          Distributed by King Features Syndicate, Inc.

Library of Congress Catalog Card Number: 89-91416

ISBN 0-449-13381-8

Manufactured in the United States of America

First Edition: December 1989
Third Printing: February 1991

"Hi, love! I'd give you a kiss,
but there doesn't seem to be any
room for it."

"PJ won't run away from home. He can't reach the doorknob."

"There used to be a tree on this platform."

"Aw — did you hurt yourself, Honey?
Come over here. I'll feel sorry
for you."

"Just in case you got breakfast in bed,
Mommy, how would you want all
your eggs cooked!"

"Daddy, why don't you sing when you come home from work like Mr. Rogers does?"

"Cross my heart and hope to . . .
Well — get a little sick."

"You're supposed to be leading, PJ!"

"Barfy's tail can only give half a wag
when he's lying down."

"Mommy said 'We'll see.' That
means 'no.'"

"PJ's lucky. He doesn't have to save his
clothes and toys for anybody."

"How come Billy was born in a different outfit than me?"

"The skin on this bread is too tough."

"That plane learned how to blink its lights from the lightning bugs."

"Everybody's friendly when Mommy's
driving. They all blow their
horns at us."

"I like screen doors. Flies can't go
through them, but your
voice can."

"This robot is old-fashioned. It doesn't fold up into anything."

"PJ can speak a foreign language! He's
sayin' stuff I can't understand."

"Daddy, will you tie this pretzel
into the bow kind?"

"Do you think I need a soda transfusion?"

"Daddy, your little radio is dead
so we buried it."

"Why doesn't she answer her beeper?"

"When I was a boy bikes didn't have upholstery."

"The part Daddy likes best about runnin'
three miles is tellin' people about it."

"Mommy, can we have croissants
for breakfast?"

"My mom wants to know if I could switch
to the outfield."

"Who kept picking up the extension while
I was on the phone?"
"Not me." "Not me!"

"I wouldn't want to be a mermaid. How would you ride a bike?"

"The sticky stuff's lemonade and the crunchy stuff's the sugar."

"But I'm not sleepin'. Only my
eyes are."

"Fireflies don't come out when it's raining 'cause it would put their fires out."

"Mommy, remember that book you had to
pay the library for last year?"

"When I grow up I wanna be a vegetarian!"

"Hey, Billy! How's
Mary Ann?"

"I'd like to have him if I was 'it'
for hide-and-seek."

"Oh, oh! There's Mommy at the scream door!"

"Daddy, could you fix my lightning bug? It doesn't work anymore!"

"You're early, Daddy. Did you work undertime?"

"Kittycat is walking tall!"

"Do they have the scarecrow and
the cowardly lion, too?"

"Wanna hear yourself snore?"

"The FBI has over 75 million fingerprints."
"So do we."

"You only add one can of water for soup.
Three cans are for frozen juice."

"Whenever the breeze blows the daisies
do their exercises."

"But, I CAN'T stop crying! My eyes
are too full of tears!"

"I don't want to hear anymore
Popeye imitations."

"If you've never seen a purple cow
here's your chance."

"I like dogs 'cause if you're doing
something stupid they don't yell
at you. They do it with you."

"The magic word is 'please,' not 'abracadabra.' "

"Surf's up, Mommy!"

"Cows eat plain grass and people eat
SPARROW GRASS."

"WE FINALLY WON ONE!"   "The other team didn't show up."

"We just wanted to see which one had
the best horn."

"PJ's touching it, Daddy! Does that mean
we hafta buy it now?"

"Lee Iacocca stands behind every
car we sell."

"TRADE-IN? We're not gonna get rid of
our good OLD car, are we?"

"If we wash our face and hands and promise
not to touch anything can we ALL take
a test drive?"

"Why does his boss hide in another room?"

"Are you sure you know how to drive a
mini-van, Daddy?"

"Like they say on TV: IT'S A BRA-AND
NEW CA-A-AR!"

"... And it has a slidin' door like
an elevator."

"Goodnight, Mommy!"
"Goodnight, Daddy!"

"Goodnight,
new car!"

"Let's name it Minnie! And her middle name can be Van!"

"Don't worry, Daddy. When the rain stops
we'll all help you wash it."

"Squeeze bottles have replaced
water pistols!"

"Couldn't we fix Dolly's hair like
Cyndi Lauper's?"

"Just close your mouf and don't smell."

"Mommy, will you make Billy pay up?
I stood on my head and he bet a
million dollars I couldn't do it!"

"Why does Daddy keep lookin'
at his watch?"

"Claire's 'frigerator knows how to
make ice by itself!"

"They both shake hands with me, but
I can't get them to shake hands
with each other."

"That's a quarter moon."
"I only have a dime."

"Why not, Mommy? Look at all the
firewood we gathered."

"There are peanuts in my orange."

"Daddy's pumping PJ."

"I wish it was school time so you could drive me there and everybody could see our new car!"

"Go to your room!"

"Kittycat likes dresses 'cause they make better laps."

"Billy's pushin' his ears together so
he can't hear me."

"Go ahead, ask her. My mom can tell ya
exactly how many days till school
starts without even lookin'
at a calendar."

"Could you shave the fur off
this peach?"

"WOW! That angel must've bowled
a STRIKE!"

"Can you help me find a grape flavor crayon?"

"Before you go on vacation you have
your mail disconnected."

"We'll be away for 41 meals."

"We ought to be getting more than
25 miles per litter bag!"

"I'm makin' a list of all the states
we see on license plates. I've
got 49 to go."

"See if we can get one near the
ice machine."

"Can we stay here a few days, Mommy? I
just made a new friend."

"I don't even HAFTA see out! I know
we're close to the ocean 'cause
my LIPS are salty!"

"The sand's
too hot!"

"The water's
too cold!"

"I love beaches 'cause there's always
an ocean near them!"

"Remember, Jeffy, it's PJ's ocean, too!"

"I'm glad they put the shallow end
closest to the beach!"

"Some ocean got stuck in his ear."

"Next time I think we should bring
more candy bars and Mommy!"

"He's still break-dancing."

"It's too hot out there. I'm gonna
stay indoors."

"Daddy! Your stuffing's coming out!"

"I'll borrow some ocean to fill it."

"It's not an octopus, it's a piece
of seaweed."

"Keep looking, everybody. We've got to
find the car keys."

"Why can't we see the sharp points
on the stars?"

"Mommy! There's the plane that drove us to grandma's."

"I'm brushin' my tooth real good so the
tooth fairy will be sure to take it."

"This is me in front of the bottom part
of the Washington Monument."

"When I grow up I'm gonna GO places
instead of just bein' taken."

"Who's been sitting in my chair?"

"The organ at the ballpark is more fun."

"I feel like a paper doll when you do that."

"This apple's smilin' 'cause I took a
bite out of him."

"No, Jeffy. It's not a REAL grown-up
signature unless people can't
read it."

"I wish we lived in Colorado or Wyoming.
They're the easiest states to draw."

"Would you move the car, Daddy? Our
hopscotch court is under it."

"Kittycat is putting a block on you."

"Oh-oh! I got some hand lotion on my arm."

"No more hide-and-seek in the house!
I'm tired of putting clothes
back on hangers."

"Where's your video camera, Daddy? We'll give you the TV rights to our game."

"Listen! Doesn't that make you hungry? It's Mommy getting out the dishes for dinner."

"You enjoy them even more when you realize
this childhood mini-series won't
be rerun."

"Come quick, Mommy! PJ's headed for the
'no-no, don't touch' room!"

You can have lots more fun
with
BIL KEANE and
THE FAMILY CIRCUS